A brief recognition of New-Englands errand into the wilderness : made in the audience of the General Assembly of the Massachusetts Colony at Boston in N.E. on the 11th of the third moneth, 1670, being the day of election there.

Samuel Danforth

A BRIEF
RECOGNITION
OF
NEW-ENGLANDS
ERRAND
INTO THE
Wilderneſs;

Made in the Audience of the General Aſſembly of the
Maſſachuſets Colony, at *Boſton* in *N. E.* on the
11ʰ of the third Moneth, 1670. being the

DAY of ELECTION
THERE.

By *Samuel Danforth*, Paſtor of the Church of
Chriſt in *Roxbury* in *N. E.*

Jer. 2. 2. *Go, and cry in the ears of Jeruſalem, ſaying Thus ſaith the Lord, I
remember thee, the kindneſs of thy youth, the love of thine eſpouſals,
when thou wenteſt after me in the Wilderneſs, in a Land that was not
ſown*

3 *Iſrael was Holineſs unto the Lord, and the firſt-fruits of his increaſe——*
5 *Thus ſaith the Lord, What iniquity have your fathers found in me, that
the are gone far from me, and have walked after vanity, and are become vain* ?

CAMBRIDGE:
Printed by *S. G.* and *M F.*   1 6 7 1.

Chriſtian Reader,

A Word ſpoken in due ſeaſon (ſaith Solomon) how good is it? *Prov* 15 23. *And again,* A word fitly ſpoken is like Apples of gold in pictures of ſilver, *Chap.*25. 11. *Such were the words of our Lord Jeſus, who (accommodating himſelf to the Way of Doctrine uſed by in ſe Eaſtern Nations) did by Parabolical diſcourſes delight to breathe forth the deep Myſteries of divine and heavenly wiſdome. And how plain, but pungent, his Sermons were, how perſpicuous, yet unſpeakably profound were thoſe Oracles which flowed out of his lips of grace, none are ignorant, who are not unacquainted with what the holy Evangeliſts do harmoniouſly relate concerning him. No more excellent Patern then the Lord Jeſus for the Miniſtry of the New Teſtament to imitate: And of all the words of the Sacred Scripture (though all are of equal Authority, as being of the Canon, yet) none ſeems to have a more eminent immediation of Heart-commanding virtue, then thoſe which proceeded directly out of the mouth of the Lord himſelf, whereof this Text is one, upon which the following Sermon is ſpent. And how much of the Spirit of our Saviour appears therein, I need not ſay, and which perhaps will not, at the firſt daſh, be diſcerned by the ordinary or curſory Reader, but Wiſdome is juſtified of her children. The ſeaſonableneſs, and ſuitableneſs of this work which is now in thine hand, unto our preſent Wilderneſs ſtate, will commend it ſelf unto the judicious Chriſtian, whoſe heart doth indeed travel with the labouring Intereſt of the Kingdome of our Lord Jeſus in theſe Ends of the Earth. The Text carrying with it ſo much heavenly argumentation, being ſo profitable for Doctrine, for Reproof, for Correction, for Inſtruction in righteouſneſs, as though intended by our Lord Jeſus for ſuch a Way as that, whereon this Sermon was Preached, (and alſo before ſuch an Auditory). Whoſo applauds the former, will not diſprove the latter, the Reverend Author*

thereof

To the Christian Reader.

thereof, observing therein the Saying of that Apostolick Man of God (and very judicious in his Advice to younger Ministers about such matters) his most Reverend Father of blessed Memory, Mr. Wilson, viz. That he delighted in such a Sermon wherein the Preacher kept close unto his Text, and the proper scope thereof, and wandered not from it by needless excursions, and impertinent enlargements.

The loss of first love, first to Christ, and so to the Subjects, and Order of his Kingdome, being a Radical Disease too tremendously growing upon so great a part of the Body of Professors in this Land, unto a Laodicean lukewarmness in the matters of God, notwithstanding the signal, and unparallel Experiences of the blessing of God upon this people, a people so often saved by the Lord in the Way of Moses and Aaron's meeting, and kissing one another in the Mount of God, and the observation of that Declension justly calling for so meet an Antidote and faithful Caution, as is the ensuing Sermon (οὐκ ἐν πειθοῖς ἀνθρωπίνης σοφίας λόγοις, ἀλλ' ἐν ἀποδείξει Πνεύματος ᴋ, δυνάμεως) unto such, to review, and consider in earnest their Errand into this Wilderness: and the recovery of their affections to the Name of Christ, in the chastity, vigour, and fervour thereof, by a thorough-Reformation of things in the Matters of his Worship, being a special duty in this hour of Temptation incumbent, as on the Magistracy in their Sphere, so on the Ministry in theirs, whereby they may declare themselves loyal to Christ in their Generation-work, hath no doubt inclined the heart of this Servant of his, to yield unto the Perswasions of divers, that these his Meditations might be published, and so (through the blessing of God) advance that desired Reformation. It is not a loose Toleration, nor a rigid Independent-Separation, but an holy, and brotherly Reformation which all should in such an hour be endeavouring. And how perillous a Sceptical Indifferency, or a Reed-like Vacillation, much more wilful Opposition to the Doctrine and Way of the first Fathers and Founders of this Colony in Matters of Religion, would be, were it onely in those two Points about the Magistrates Coercive Power in Matters of Religion, (contrary to that Toleration aforesaid) and about Communion of Churches in Synods, &c. described also by them, from the Word

of

To the Christian Reader.

of God, in the Platform of Discipline *(contrary to that Indepen-dent-Separation aforesaid)* will be evident to those that understand *what these things mean,* scil. 1. Quod liberi sunt Spirituales à jugo potestatis secularis : *and* 2. Quod Ecclesia non potest er-rare. *It is said I remember (*Josh. 24. 31.) *that* Israel *served the* Lord *all the dayes of* Joshua, *and all the dayes of the* Elders *that out-lived* Joshua, *and which had known all the works of the* Lord *that he had done for* Israel : *It is much to* Israels *advantage in the service of God, when the Lord graciously continues those, who are acquainted with the* First Wayes *of such a people, as hath been* Holiness to the Lord, *and with the* First Works *of the Lord in his laying the Foundation of that Glory which might dwell in their* Land. *And it is recorded (*Exod. 1. 8) *as an inlet to* Israels *ca-lamitous state, in that place where the Lord had greatly multiplied and blessed them, that* there arose up a New King which knew not Joseph. *When* Joseph, *or* Joshua *are unknown, or forgotten, and the work and way of God in leading his people by the hand of* Moses *and* Aaron *in their primitive Glory not understood, or not minded by these or those, how fearfully ominous to* Israel *must it needs be ! and how necessitating the affectionate repetition, again, and again, of that expostulatory, sad Interrogation of our Saviour,* But what went ye out into the Wilderness to see ? *And should there arise such another Generation (as is mentioned* Judg. 2. 11.) *after our Fathers are removed to rest from the warfare of the ser-vice of the Tabernacle of God in their Generation, as should* not know the Lord, *nor regard the works which he hath done for our* Israel, *what may be expected, but that (as the following Con-text shews)* the anger of the Lord should wax hot against Israel, *and that he deliver us also into the hand of spoilers ?* &c. *Strangers to the* FIRST *Intention of the people of God in their planting in this Wilderness, and so to the Doctrine of Faith and Order left in Print behinde them (more sure and credible then some* Unwritten Traditions *thereabout) may prove dangerous Instru-ments to* OUR *Ruine, if the Lord in mercy prevent not.*

It was the commendation of Timothy *by* Paul, 2 Tim. 3. 10, 11. *as also a profitable instruction and encouragement to him, When he saith,* But thou hast fully known my doctrine, manner of life,

A 3   purpose, purpofe, faith, long fuffering, charity, patience, perfecutions, afflictions which came unto me at Antioch, at Iconium, at Lyftra, what perfecutions I endured; but out of them all the Lord delivered me : the like may be faid of this Reverend Servant of the Lord, my dear Brother in Chrift, to whom it hath feemed good παρακληθηναι αναθω αθθω αμειβθς (according to that Word of Wifdome which is given to him by that fame holy Spirit, from whom proceed thofe diverfities of gifts, which he divides to every man feverally as he will) to leave this enfuing Teftimony of his follicitude for the poor Woman fled alfo into this wildernefs, unto the confideration of all fuch as are wife-hearted in Ifrael. His nearnefs to, and intimacy with my Ever-honoured Father now with God (he being brought up with him as a Son with a Father) commands from my Pen a glad apprehending the opportunity of performing this fervice of waiting upon it to the Prefs; praying, that the Lord would make the words thereof as Goads, and Nails faftened by the Mafters of Affemblies, and given by that one Shepherd the Lord Jefus: In Whom I am

Thine, for the fervice of thy Faith,

Thomas Shepard.

A BRIEF

✤✤✤✤✤✤✤✤✤✤✤✤✤✤✤✤✤✤✤✤✤✤✤✤)

A BRIEF
RECOGNITION
OF
New-Englands Errand into the
WILDERNESS.

Matth. 11. 7, 8, 9.

*— What went ye out into the wilderness to see ? A reed
shaken with the wind?*

*But what went ye out for to see? A man clothed in soft
raiment? behold, they that wear soft clothing, are in
Kings houses.*

*But what went ye out for to see? A Prophet ?- yea, I say
unto you, and more then a Prophet.*

THese words are our Saviour's *Proem* to his illustrious Encomium of *John* the *Baptist*. *John* began
his Ministry, not in *Jerusalem*, nor in any famous
City of *Judea*, but in the *Wilderness*, i. e. in a
woody, retired and solitary place, thereby withdrawing himself from the envy and preposterous zeal of such as were ad-
dicted to their old Traditions, and also taking the people aside
from the noise and tumult of their secular occasions and busi-
nesses, which might have obstructed their ready and cheerful
attendance unto his Doctrine. The Ministry of *John* at first
was entertained by all sorts with singular affection : There *went
out to him Jerusalem and all Judea, and all the region round about
Jordan,* Mat. 3 5. but after awhile, the people's fervour abated,
and

and *John* being kept under restraint divers moneths, his authority and esteem begin to decay and languish, *John* 5. 35. Wherefore our Saviour, taking occasion from *Johns* Messengers coming to him, after their departure, gives an excellent *Elogie* and Commendation of *John*, to the intent that He might ratifie and confirm his Doctrine and Administration, and revive his Authority and Estimation in the hearts and consciences of the people.

This *Elogie* our Saviour begins with an elegant *Dialogism*, which the Rhetorician calleth *Communication* : gravely deliberating with his Hearers, and seriously enquiring to what purpose they went out into the Wilderness, and what expectation drew them thither. Wherein we have, 1. *The general Question, and main subject of his Inquisition.* 2. *The particular Enquiries.* 3. *The Determination of the Question.*

The general Question is, *what went ye out into the Wildernss to see?* He saith not, Whom went ye out to *hear*, but what went ye out to *see?* Θεάσασθαι. The phrase agrees to Shows and Stage-playes, plainly arguing that many of those, who seemed well-affected to *John*, and flock'd after him, were *Theatrical* Hearers, *Spectators* rather then *Auditors*, they went not to *hear*, but to *see*; they went to gaze upon a new and strange Spectacle.

This general Question being propounded, the first particular Enquiry is, whether they went to see *A reed shaken with the wind?* The expression is Metaphorical and Proverbial. A reed when the season is calm, lifts up it self and stands upright, but no sooner doth the wind blow upon it, but it shakes and trembles, bends and bows down, and then gets up again : and again it yields and bows, and then lifts up it self again. A notable *Emblem* of light, empty and inconstant persons, who in times of peace and tranquility, give a fair and plausible Testimony to the Truth; but no sooner do the winds of Temptation blow upon them, and the waves of Troubles roll over them, but they incline and yield to the prevailing Party : but when the Tempest is over, they recover themselves and assert the Truth again. The meaning then of this first Enquiry is, Went ye out

into

into the Wildernefs to fee a light, vain and inconstant man, one that could confefs and deny, and deny and confefs the fame Truth? This Interrogation is to be understood negatively and ironical'y, q d. Surely ye went not into the defert to behold fuch a ludicrous and ridiculous fight, *A man like unto a reed fhaken with the wind.* Under the negation of the contrary levity, our Saviour fets forth one of *John's* excellencies, viz. his eminent *Conftancy* in afferting the Truth. The winds of various temptations both on the right hand and on the left, blew upon him, yet he wavered not in his teftimony concerning Chrift, *He confeffed and denied not, but confeffed the truth.*

Then, the general Queftion is repeated, *But what went ye out for to fee?* and a fecond particular Enquiry made, Was it to fee *a man clothed in foft raiment?* This Interrogation hath alfo the force of a negation, q.d. Surely ye went not into the Wildernefs to fee a man clothed in filken and coftly Apparel. The reafon of this is added, *Behold, they that wear foft clothing, are in Kings houfes.* Delicate and coftly Apparel is to be expected in Princes Courts, and not in wilde Woods and Forrefts. Under the negation of *John's* affectation of Courtly delicacy, our Saviour fets forth another of *John's* excellencies, viz. his frugal *gravity* and *fobriety,* who wore rough garments, and lived on courfe and mean fare, *Mat 3 4* which aufteere kinde of life was accommodated to the place and work of his Miniftry. *John* Preached in the Wildernefs, which was no fit place for filken and foft raiment. His work was to prepare a people for the Lord, by calling them off from worldly pomp and vanities, unto repentance and mourning for fin. His peculiar habit and diet was fuch as became a penitentiary Preacher.

Thirdly, the generall Queftion is reiterated, *But what went ye out for to fee?* and a third particular Enquiry made, Was it to fee *a Prophet?* This Interrogation is to be underftood affirmatively, q d no doubt but it was to fee a *Prophet.* Had not *John* been a rare and excellent Minifter of God, you would never have gone out of your Cities into the defert to have feen him. Thus our Saviour fets forth another of *John's* admirable excellencies, viz. his *Prophetical Office* and Function. *John* was not an ordinary Interpreter of the Law, much less a Teacher of Jewish Traditions, but *a Prophet,* one who by the extraordinary Inspiration of the holy Ghost, made known the Mysteries of Salvation, *Luke* 1. 76,77.

Lastly, our Saviour determines and concludes the Question, He, whom ye went out to see was *more then a 'Prophet,* περι αντερον προφητε, *much more,* or *abundantly more then a Prophet.* This he confirms by his wonted Asseveration, *Yea, I say unto you,* and much more then a Prophet. How was *John* much more then a Prophet? *John* was *Chrisst Herauld* sent immediately before his face, to proclaim his Coming and Kingdome, and prepare the people for the reception of him by the Baptism of Repentance, *ver.*10. Hence it follows *ver.*11. *Among all that are born of women, there hath not risen a greater Prophet then John.* *John* was greater then any of the Prophets that were before him, not in respect of his personal graces and virtues, (for who shall perswade us that he excelled *Abraham* in the grace of *Faith,* who was the father of the faithful, or *Moses* in *Meekness,* who was the meekest man on earth, or *David* in *Faithfulness,* who was a man after Gods own heart, or *Solomon* in *wisdome,* who was the wisest man that ever was or shall be ?) but in respect of the manner of his dispensation. All the *Prophets* foretold Chrisst Coming, his Sufferings and Glory, but the *Baptist* was his *Harbinger* and *Forerunner,* that bare the Sword before him, Proclaimed his Presence, and made room for him in the hearts of the people. All the *Prophets* saw Christ afar off, but the *Baptist* saw him present, baptized him, and applied the Types to him personally. *Behold the Lamb of God. He saw and bare record that this is the Son of God,* Joh. 1.29,34. *But he that is least in the Kingdome of Heaven, is greater then John.* The least Prophet in the Kingdome of Heaven, *i.e.* the least Minister of the Gospel since Chrisst's Ascension, is greater then *John,* not in respect of the measure of his personal gifts, nor in respect of the manner of his Calling, but in respect of the *Object* of his Ministry, *Christ on the Throne,* having finished the work of our Redemption, and in respect of the *degree* of the revelation of Christ, which is far more clear and full. *John*
shewed

ſhewed Chriſt in the fleſh, and pointed to him with his finger, but the Miniſters f the Goſpel declare that he hath done and ſuffered all things neceſſary to our Salvation, and is riſen again and ſet down at the right hand of God.

Doct. Such as have ſometime left their pleaſant Cities and Habitations to enjoy the pure Worſhip of God in a Wilderneſs, are apt in time to abate and cool in their affection thereunto. but then the Lord calls upon them ſeriouſly and throughly to examine themſelves, what it was that drew them into the wilderneſs, and to conſider that it was not the expectation of ludicrous levity, nor of Courtly pomp and delicacy, but of the free and clear diſpenſation of the Goſpel and Kingdome of God.

This Doctrine conſiſts of two diſtinct Branches; let me open them ſeverally.

Branch 1. *Such as have ſometime left their pleaſant Cities and Habitations, to enjoy the pure Worſhip of God in a Wildernesſ, are apt in time to abate and cool in their affection thereunto.* To what pui poſe did the Children of *Iſrael* leave their Cities and Houſes in *Egypt*, and go forth into the Wildernesſ? was it not to *hold a Feaſt to the Lord*, and to *ſacrifice to the God of their fathers?* That was the onely reaſon, which they gave of their motion to *Pharaoh, Exod.*5.1,3. but how ſoon did they forget their Errand into the Wildernesſ, and corrupt themſelves in their own Inventions? within a few moneths after their coming out of *Egypt, they make a Calf in Horeb, and worſhip the molten Image, and change their glory into the ſimilitude of an Ox that eateth graſs, Pſal.*106.19,20. *Exod.*32 7,8. yea for the ſpace of forty years in the Wildernesſ, while they pretended to Sacrifice to the Lord, they indeed worſhipped the Stars and the Hoſt of Heaven, and together with the Lords Tabernacle, carried about with them the Tabernacle of *Moloch, Amos* 5.25,26. *Acts* 7.42,43. And how did they ſpend their time in the Wildernesſ, but in tempting God, and in murmuring againſt their godly and faithful Teachers and Rulers, *Moſes* and *Aaron?* Pſal.95 8. To what purpoſe did the Children of the Captivity upon *Cyrus* his Proclamation, leave their Houſes which they had built, and their Vineyards and Oliveyards which they had planted in the Province of *Baby-lon*, and return to *Judea* and *Jerusalem*, which were now become a Wilderness? was it not that they might build the House of God at *Jerusalem*, and set up the Temple-worship? But how shamefully did they neglect that great and honourable Work for the space of above forty years? They pretended that Gods time was not come to build his House, because of the rubs and obstructions which they met with, whereas all their difficulties and discouragements hindred not their building of stately houses for themselves, *Hag.* 1 2,3,4. To what purpose did *Jerusalem* & all *Judea*,& all the region round about *Jordan*,leave their several Cities and Habitations, and flock into the *wilderness of Judea?* was it not to see that *burning and shining light,* which God had raised up? To hear his heavenly Doctrine, and partake of that new Sacrament, which he administred? O how they were affected with his rare and excellent gifts! with his clear, lively and powerful Ministry! *The Kingdome of Heaven pressed in* upon them *with* a holy *violence, and the violent,* the zealous and affectionate hearers of the Gospel, *took it by force,* Mat.11.12. Luk.16.16. They leapt over all discouragements and impediments, whether outward, as Legal Rites and Ceremonies, or inward, the sense of their own sin and unworthiness, and press'd into the Kingdome of God, as men rush into a Theatre to see a pleasant Sight, or as Souldiers run into a besieged City, to take the Spoil thereof: but their hot fit is soon over, their affection lasted but for an *hour,* i e a short season, *Joh.*5.35.

Reas. 1. Because the *affection* of many to the Ministry of the Gospel and the pure Worship of God, is built upon *temporary* and *transitory* grounds, as the *novelty* and *strangeness of the matter, the rareness and excellency of Ministerial Gifts, the voice of the people, the countenance of great men, and the hope of worldly advantage.* The Jews had lien in ignorance and darkness a long time, being trained up under the superstitious observances of their old Traditions, which were vain, empty and unprofitable Customes, and the Church wanted the gift of Prophecy about four hundred years, and therefore when *John* the *Baptist* arose like a bright and burning light, shining amongst them with admirable

mirable gifts of the Spirit, and extraordinary feverity and gravity of manners, proclaiming the Coming and Kingdome of the Meffias, (which had been oft promifed and long expected) and preffing the people to Repentance and good works, O how they admire and reverence him? efpecially; when grown popular, and countenanced by *Herod* the *Tetrarch*. What fweet affections are kindled! what great expectations are raifed! what ravifhing joy is conceived! Hoping (as its probable) to make ufe of his Authority to caft off the *Roman* yoke, and recover their Civil Liberties, Riches and Honours. But after a little acquaintance with *John*, (for he was a publick Preacher but a year and half) his Doctrine, Adminiftrations and Prophetical Gifts, grew common and ftale things, and of little efteem with them; efpecially, when they faw their carnal hopes fruftrated, the Rulers difaffected, and *Herods* countenance and carriage toward him changed.

Reaf. 2. Becaufe *Prejudices* and *Offences* are apt to arife in the hearts of many againft the *faithful Difpenfers* of the Gofpel. The *Pharifees* and *Lawyers* came among others to the Baptifm of *John*, but when they hear his fharp reprehenfions of their *Viperous* Opinions and Practices, they naufeate his Doctrine, repudiate his Baptifm, calumniate his Converfation, *Luke* 7.30. *Herodias* hath an inward grudge and a quarrel againft him, becaufe he found fault with her inceftuous Marriage, *Mar* 6. 19, Yea, that very Age and Generation of the Jews, were like to a company of furly, fullen and froward children, whom no Mufick can pleafe, they neither dance after the Pipe, nor make lamentation after the mourner. They inveigh againft *John's* aufterity, faying that he was tranfported with diabolical fury, and was an enemy to humane fociety: and they do as much diftafte and abhor *Chrift's* gentlenefs and familiarity, traducing him, as being a fenfual and voluptuous perfon, given to intemperance and luxury, and a Patron and Abettor of loofenefs and profanenefs, *Mat.* 11. 16—19. Thus doth the frowardnefs and ftubbornnefs of man, refift and oppofe the wifdome and goodnefs of God, who ufeth various wayes and inftruments to compafs poor finners, but they through their folly and perfenefs

nefs.

nefs, fruftrate, difanul and abrogate the counfel of God againft themfelves.   The evil fpirit that troubled *Saul*, was quieted and allayed by the fweet Melody of *David's* Harp: but the mad and outragious fury that tranfports men againft the Truth and the Miniftry thereof, cannot be quieted and allayed by the voice of the Charmers, charm they never fo wifely.

Branch II. *When men abate and cool in their affection to the pure Worfhip of God, Which they went into the Wildernefs to enjoy, the Lord calls upon them feriously and throughly to examine themfelves, what it Was that drew them into the Wildernefs, and to confider that it was not the expectation of ludicrous levity, nor of Courtly pomp and delicacy, but of the free and clear difpenfation of the Gofpel and Kingdome of God.*   Our Saviour knowing that the people had loft their firft love and fingular affection to the revelation of his grace by the Miniftry of his Herauld *John*, He is very intenfe in examining them, what expectation drew them into the Wildernefs: He doth not once nor twice, but thrice propound that Queftion, *What went ye out into the Wildernefs to fee?* Yea, in particular he enquires whether it were to fee a man that was like to *a Reed fhaken with the wind?* or whether it were to fee *a man clothed like a Courtier*, or whether it were to fee a *Prophet*, and then determines the Queftion, concluding that it was to fee a great and excellent Prophet, and that had not they feen rare and admirable things in him, they would never have gone out into the Wildernefs unto him.

The Reafon is, Becaufe the ferious confideration of the ineftimable grace and mercy of God in the free and clear difpenfation of the Gofpel and Kingdome of God, is a fpecial means to convince men of their folly and perverfenefs in undervaluing the fame, and a fanctified remedy to recover their affections thereunto.   The Lord forefeeing the defection of *Ifrael* after *Mofes* his death, commands him to write that Prophetical Song, recorded in *Deut.* 32. as a Teftimony againft them: wherein the chief remedy, which he prefcribes for the prevention and healing of their Apoftacy, is their calling to remembrance Gods great and fignal love in manifefting himfelf to them in the Wildernefs, in conducting them fafely and mercifully,

cifully, and giving them poffeffion of their promifed Inheritance, *ver.* 7——14. And when *Ifrael* was apoftatized and fallen, the Lord to convince them of their ingratitude and folly, brings to their remembrance his deliverance of them out of *Egypt*, his leading them through the Wildernefs for the fpace of forty years, and not onely giving them poffeffion of their Enemies Land, but alfo raifing up, even of their own Sons, *Prophets*, faithful and eminent Minifters, and of their young men *Nazarites*, who being feparated from worldly delights and encumbrances, were Paterns of Purity and Holinefs. all which were great and obliging mercies. Yea, the Lord appeals to their own Confciences, whether thefe his favours were not real and fignal, *Amos* 2.10,11. The Prophet *Jeremiah*, that he might reduce the people from their backflidings, cries in the ears of *Jerufalem*, with earneftnefs and boldnefs declaring unto them, that the Lord remembred how well they ftood affected towards him, when he firft chofe them to be his people and efpoufed them to himfelf, how they followed him in the Wildernefs, and kept clofe to him in their long and wearifome paffage through the uncultured Defert; how they were then confecrated to God, and fet apart for his Worfhip and Service; as the firft-fruits are wont to be fequeftred and devoted to God: and thereupon expoftulates with them for their forfaking the Lord, and following after their Idols, *Jer* 2. 2,3,5,6. Surely our Saviour's *Dialogifm* with his Hearers in my Text, is not a meer Rhetorical Elegancy to adorn his Teftimony concerning *John*, but a clear and ftrong conviction of their folly in flighting and defpifing that which they fometime fo highly pretended unto, and a wholefome admonition and direction how to recover their primitive affection to his Doctrine and Adminiftration.

USE I. Of folemn and ferious Enquiry to us all in this general Affembly, Whether we have not in a great meafure forgotten our Errand into the Wildernefs. You have folemnly profeffed before God, Angels and Men, that the Caufe of your leaving your Country, kindred and Fathers houfes, and tranfporting your felves with your Wives, Little Ones

and

and Substance over the vast Ocean into this waste and howling Wilderness, was *your Liberty to walk in the Faith of the Gospel with all good Conscience according to the Order of the Gospel, and your enjoyment of the pure Worship of God according to his Institution, without humane Mixtures and Impositions.* Now let us sadly consider whether our ancient and primitive affections to the Lord Jesus, his glorious Gospel, his pure and spiritual Worship and the Order of his House, remain, abide and continue firm, constant, entire and inviolate. Our Saviour's reiteration of this Question, *What went ye out into the wilderness to see?* is no idle repetition, but a sad conviction of our dulness and backwardness to this great duty, and a clear demonstration of the weight and necessity thereof. It may be a grief to us to be put upon such an Inquisition; as it is said of *Peter,* Joh 21.17. *Peter was grieved, because he said unto him the third time, Lovest thou me?* but the Lord knoweth that a strict and rigid examination of our hearts in this point, is no more then necessary. Wherefore let us call to remembrance the former dayes, and consider whether *it was not then better with us, then it is now.*

In our first and best times the Kingdome of Heaven brake in upon us with a holy violence, and every man pressed into it. What mighty efficacy and power had the clear and faithful dispensation of the Gospel upon your hearts? how affectionately and zealously did you entertain the Kingdome of God? How careful were you, even all sorts, young and old, high and low, to take hold of the opportunities of your spiritual good and edification? ordering your secular affairs (which were wreathed and twisted together with great variety) so as not to interfere with your general Calling, but that you might *attend upon the Lord without distraction.* How diligent and faithful in preparing your hearts for the reception of the Word, *laying apart all filthiness and superfluity of naughtiness, that you might receive with meekness the ingraffed word, which is able to save your souls, and purging out all malice, guile, hypocrisies, envies, and all evil speakings, and as new-born babes, desiring the sincere milk of the Word, that ye might grow thereby?* How attentive in

hearing

hearing the everlasting Gospel, *watching daily at the gates of Wisdome, and waiting at the posts of her doors, that ye might finde eternal life, and obtain favour of the Lord?* Gleaning day by day in the field of Gods Ordinances, even among the Sheaves, and gathering up handfuls, which the Lord let fall of purpose for you, and at night going home and beating out what you had gleaned, by Meditation, Repetition, Conference, and therewith feeding your selves and your families. How painful were you in recollecting, repeating and discoursing of what you heard, whetting the Word of God upon the hearts of your Children, Servants and Neighbours? How fervent in Prayer to Almighty God for his divine Blessing upon the Seed sown, that it might take root and fructifie? O what a reverent esteem had you in those dayes of Christ's faithful Ambassadors, that declared unto you the Word of Reconciliation! *How beautiful were the feet of them, that preached the Gospel of peace, and brought the glad tidings of Salvation!* you esteemed them highly in love for their works sake. Their Persons, Names and Comforts were precious in your eyes; you counted your selves blessed in the enjoyment of a Pious, Learned and Orthodox Ministry: and though you ate the bread of adversity and drank the water of affliction, yet you rejoyced in this, that your eyes saw your Teachers, they were not removed into corners, and your ears heard a word behinde you, saying, This is the way, walk ye in it, when you turned to the right hand and when you turned to the left, *Isa* 30. 20, 21. What earnest and ardent desires had you in those dayes after Communion with Christ in the holy Sacraments? *With desire you desired* to partake of the Seals of the Covenant. You thought your Evidences for Heaven not sure nor authentick, unless the Broad Seals of the Kingdome were annexed. What solicitude was there in those dayes to *seek the Lord after the right Order?* What searching of the holy Scriptures, what Collations among your Leaders, both in their private Meetings and publick Councils and Synods, to finde out the Order, which Christ hath constituted and establish'd in his House? What fervent zeal was there then against Sectaries and Hereticks, and all manner of Heterodoxies? *You could*

C

not bear them that were evil, but tried them that pretended to
New Light and Revelations, and found them *liars.* What pious
Care was there of *Sister-Churches*, that those that wanted
Breasts, might be supplied, and that those that wanted *Peace*,
their Dissentions might be healed? What readiness was there
in those dayes to call for the help of Neighbour-Elders and Bre-
thren, in case of any Difference or Division that could not be
healed at home? What reverence was there then of the Sen-
tence of a Council, as being *decisive* and issuing the Contro-
versie? According to that ancient Proverbial Saying, *They shall
surely ask counsel at Abel, and so they ended the matter,* 2 Sam.
20.18. What holy Endeavours were there in those dayes to
propagate Religion to your Children and Posterity, training
them up in the nurture and admonition of the Lord, keeping
them under the awe of government, restraining their enormi-
ties and extravagancies, charging them to know the God of
their fathers, and serve him with a perfect heart and willing
minde; and publickly asserting and maintaining their interest
in the Lord and in his holy Covenant, and zealously opposing
those that denied the same?

And then had the Churches *rest* throughout the several Colonies, and were *edified: and walking in the fear of the Lord,
and in the comfort of the holy Ghost, were multiplied.* O how your
Faith grew exceedingly! you proceeded from faith to faith,
from a less to a greater degree and measure, growing up in
Him, who is our Head, and receiving abundance of grace and
of the gift of righteousness, that you might reign in life by Jesus Christ. O how your *Love and Charity* towards each other
abounded! O what comfort of Love! what bowels and mercies! what affectionate care was there one of another! what a
holy Sympathy in Crosses and Comforts, weeping with those
that wept, and rejoycing with those that rejoyced!

But who is there left among you, that saw these Churches *in
their first glory,* and how do you see them *now?* Are they not
in your eyes in comparison thereof, *as nothing? How is the
gold become dim! how is the most fine gold changed!* Is not the
Temper, Complexion and Countenance of the Churches
                                                    strangely

strangely altered? Doth not a careless, remiss, flat, dry, cold, dead frame of spirit, grow in upon us secretly, strongly, prodigiously? They that have Ordinances, are as though they had none; and they that hear the Word, as though they heard it not; and they that pray, as though they prayed not; and they that receive Sacraments, as though they received them not; and they that are exercised in the holy things, using them by the by, as matters of custome and ceremony, so as not to hinder their eager profecution of other things which their hearts are set upon. Yea and in some particular Congregations amongst us, is there not *in stead of a sweet smell, a stink? and in stead of a girdle, a rent? and in stead of a stomacher, a girding with sackcloth? and burning in stead of beauty? yea the Vineyard is all overgrown with thorns, and nettles cover the face thereof, and the stone wall thereof is broken down,* Prov.24 31. yea, and that which is the most sad and certain sign of calamity approaching, *Iniquity aboundeth, and the love of many waxeth cold,* Mat.24 12. Pride, Contention, Worldliness, Covetousness, Luxury, Drunkenness and Uncleanness break in like a flood upon us, and good men grow cold in their love to God and to one another. If a man be cold in his bed, let them lay on the more clothes, that he may get heat: but we are like to *David* in his old age, *they covered him with clothes, but he gat no heat,* 2 Sam.1.1. The Lord heaps mercies, favours, blessings upon us, and loads us daily with his benefits, but all his love and bounty cannot heat and warm our hearts and affections. Well, the furnace is able to heat and melt the coldest Iron: but how oft hath the Lord cast us into the hot furnace of Affliction and Tribulation, and we have been scorched and burnt, yet not melted, but hardened thereby, *Isa.*63 17. How long hath God kept us in the furnace day after day, moneth after moneth, year after year? but all our Afflictions, Crosses, Trials have not been able to keep our hearts in a warm temper.

Now let me freely deliberate with you, what may be the *Causes* and *Grounds* of *such decayes and languishings* in our affections to, and estimation of that which we came into the Wildernefs to enjoy? Is it because *there is no bread, neither is there* any water, and our foul loatheth this light bread? Numb.21.5. Our foul is dried away, and there is nothing at all, besides this *Manna*, before our eyes, Numb.11.6. What, is Manna no bread? Is this Angelical food, light bread, which cannot satisfie, but starves the Soul? Doth our Soul loath the bread of Heaven? The Lord be merciful to us. The full foul loatheth the honey-comb, *Prov.27.7.*

What then is the cause of our decayes and languishings? Is it because the Spirit of the Lord is straitned and limited in the dispensers of the Gospel, and hence our joyes and comforts are lessened and shortned? *O thou that art named the house of Jacob, is the Spirit of the Lord straitned? are those his doings? Do n't my words do good to him that walketh uprightly?* Mic.2.7. Surely it is not for want of fulness in the Spirit of God, that he with-holds comforts and blessings from any; neither doth he delight in threatnings and judgements, but his words both promise and perform that which is good and comfortable to them that walk uprightly. The Spirit is able to enlarge it self unto the reviving and cheering of every man's heart; and that should we experience, did not our iniquity put a barre. 2 Cor.6.11,12. *O ye Corinthians, our mouth is open unto you, our heart is enlarged: Ye are not straitned in us, but ye are straitned in your own bowels.* The Spirit of God dilateth and enlargeth the heart of the faith-full Ministry for the good of the people; but many times the people are straitned in their own bowels, and cannot receive such a large portion, as the Lord hath provided for them. *What then is the cause of our coolings, faintings and languishings?* The ground and principal cause is our *Unbelief:* We believe not the Grace and Power of God in Christ. Where is that lively exercise of faith, which ought to be, in our attendance upon the Lord in his holy Ordinances? Christ came to *Nazareth* with his heart full of love and compassion, and his hands full of blessings to bestow upon his old Acquaintance and Neigh-bours, among whom he had been brought up, but their *Unbelief* restrained his tender mercies, and bound his Omnipotent hands, that he could not do any great or illustrious Miracle a-mongst them. *Mat.13.58. Mark 6.5,6. He could do there no*
                                                              mighty

mighty work— *and he marvelled because of their unbelief.* Unbelief ftraitens the grace and power of Chrift, and hinders the communication of divine favours and fpecial mercies. The word preached profits not, when it is not mixed with faith in them that hear it, *Heb.* 4.2 We may pray earneftly, but if we ask not in faith, how can we expect to receive any thing of the Lord ? *Jam* 1.6,7.

But though Unbelief be the principal, yet it is not the fole caufe of our decayes and languifhings : *Inordinate worldly Cares, predominent Lufts, and malignant Paffions and Diftempers* ftifle and choak the Word, and quench our affections to the Kingdome of God, *Luke* 8 14. The Manna was gathered early in the morning, when the Sun waxed hot, it melted, *Exod.* 16. 21. It was a fearful Judgement on *Dathan* and *Abiram,* that the earth opened its mouth and fwallowed them up. How many Profeffors of Religion, are fwallowed up alive by earthly affections ? Such as efcape the *Lime-pit of Pharifaical Hypocrifie,* fall into the *Coal-pit of Sadducean Atheifm and Epicurifm* Pharifaifm and Sadduceifm do almoft divide the Profeffing World between them. Some fplit upon the *Rock* of affected oftentation of fingular Piety and Holinefs, and others are drawn into the *Whirpool,* and perifh in the *Gulf* of Senfuality and Luxury.

If any queftion how feafonable fuch a Difcourfe may be upon fuch a Day, as this, let him confider, *Hag.* 2. 10—14. *In the four and twentieth day of the ninth moneth, in the fecond year of Darius, came the word of the Lord by Haggai the Prophet, faying, Thus faith the Lord of Hofts, Ask now the Priefts corcerning the law, faying, If one bear holy flefh in the skirt of his garment, and with his skirt do touch bread, or pottage, or wine, or oyl, or any meat, shall it be holy ? And the Priefts anfwered and faid, No. Then faid Haggai, If one that is unclean by a dead body, touch any of thefe, shall it be unclean ? And the Priefts anfwered and faid, It shall be unclean Then anfwered Haggai and faid, So is this people, and fo is this nation before me, faith the Lord, and fo is every work of their hands, and that which they offer there is unclean* It was an high and great day, wherein

the

the Prophet spake these words, and an holy and honourable Work, which the people were employed in. For this day they laid the Foundation of the Lords Temple, *v r* 18. nevertheless, the Lord saw it necessary this very day to represent and declare unto them, the pollution and uncleanness both of their persons and of their holy Services, that they might be deeply humbled before God, and carry on their present Work more holy and purely. What was their uncleanness? Their eager pursuit of their private Interests, took off their hearts and affections from the affairs of the House of God. It seems they pleased themselves with this, that the Altar stood upon its Bases, and Sacrifices were daily offered thereon, and the building of the Temple was onely deferred untill a fit opportunity were afforded, free from disturbance and opposition; and having now gained such a season, they are ready to build the Temple: but the Lord convinceth them out of the Law, that their former negligence was not expiated by their daily Sacrifices, but the guilt thereof rendred both the *Nation* and this *holy and honourable Work*, which they were about, *vile and unclean* in the sight of God. And having thus shewn them their spiritual uncleanness, he encourageth them to go on with the work in hand, the building of the Temple, promising them from *this day* to bless them, *ver* 18.

USE II. Of Exhortation, To excite and stir us all up to attend and prosecute our Errand into the Wilderness. *To what purpose came we into this place, and what expectation drew us hither?* Surely, not the expectation of *ludicrous Levity.* We came not hither to see *a Reed shaken with the wind.* Then let not us be *Reeds*, light, empty, vain, hollow-hearted Professors, shaken with every wind of Temptation: but solid, serious and sober Christians, constant and stedfast in the Profession and Practice of the Truth, *Trees of Righteousness, the planting of the Lord, that he may be glorified,* holding fast the profession of our Faith without wavering.

Alas, there is such variety and diversity of Opinions and Judgements, that we know not what to believe.

Were there not as various and different Opinions touching
the

the Perſon of Chriſt, even in the dayes of his fleſh? Some ſaid that He was *John the Baptiſt,* ſome *Elias,* others *Jeremias,* or one of the old *Prophets.* Some ſaid he was a gluttonous man, and a wine-bibber, a friend of publicans and ſinners, others ſaid He was a *Samaritan,* and had a Devil, yet the Diſciples knew what to believe. *Whom ſay ye that I am? Thou art Chriſt, the Son of the living God,* Mat 16.15,16. The various heterodox Opinions of the people, ſerve as a *foil* or tinctured leaf to ſet off the luſtre and beauty of the Orthodox and Apoſtolical Faith. This is truly commendable, when in ſuch variety and diverſity of Apprehenſions, you are not byaſſed by any ſiniſter reſpects, but diſcern, embrace and profeſs the Truth, as it is in Chriſt Jeſus.

But to what purpoſe came we into the Wilderneſs, and what expectation drew us hither? Not the expectation of *Courtly Pomp and Delicacy.* We came not hither to ſee men clothed like *Courtiers.* The affectation of Courtly Pomp and Gallantry, is very unſuitable in a Wilderneſs. Gorgeous Attire is comely in Princes Courts, if it exceed not the limits of Chriſtian Sobriety: but exceſs in Kings houſes, eſcapes not divine Vengeance. Zeph. 1.8. —— *I will puniſh the Princes and the Kings children, and all ſuch as are clothed with ſtrange Apparel.* The pride and haughtineſs of the Ladies of *Zion* in their ſuperfluous Ornaments and ſtately geſtures, brought wrath upon themſelves, upon their Husbands, and upon their Children, yea and upon the whole Land, *Iſa.*3. 16——26. How much more intolerable and abominable is exceſs of this kinde in a Wilderneſs, where we are ſo far removed from the Riches and Honours of Princes Courts?

To what purpoſe then came we into the Wilderneſs, and what expectation drew us hither? Was it not the expectation of the *pure and faithful Diſpenſation* of the Goſpel and Kingdome of God? The times were ſuch that we could not enjoy it in our own Land: and therefore having obtained *Liberty* and a gracious *Patent* from our *Soveraign,* we left our Country, Kindred and Fathers houſes, and came into theſe wilde Woods and Deſerts, where

where the Lord hath planted us, and made us *dwell in a place of our own, that we might move no more, and that the children of wickedness might not assault us any more,* 2 Sam 7.10 What is it that *distinguisheth* New-England from other Colonies and Plantations in *America?* Not our transportation over the *Atlantick* Ocean, but the *Ministry* of Gods faithful Prophets, and the fruition of his holy *Ordinances.* Did not the Lord bring *the Philistines from Caphtor, and the Assyrians from Kir,* as well as *Israel from the land of Egypt?* Amos 9.7. But *by a Prophet the Lord brought Israel out of Egypt, and by a Prophet was he preserved,* Hof. 12. 13. What, is the Price and Esteem of Gods Prophets, and their faithful Dispensations, now fallen in our hearts?

The hardships, difficulties and sufferings, which you have exposed your selves unto, that you might dwell in the House of the Lord, and leave your Little Ones under the shadow of the wings of the God of *Israel,* have not been few nor small. And shall we now withdraw our selves and our Little Ones from under those *healing wings,* and lose that full Reward, which the Lord hath in his heart and hand to bestow upon us? Did we not with *Mary* choose this for our *Part, to sit at Christs feet and hear his word?* and do we now repent of our choice, and prefer the Honours, Pleasures and Profits of the world before it? *You did run well: who doth hinder you, that you should not obey the truth?* Gal. 5.7.

Hath the Lord been wanting to us, or failed our expectation? Micah 6.3. *O my people, what have I done unto thee, and wherein have I wearied thee? testifie against me.* Jer. 2. 5. *What iniquity have your fathers found in me, that they are gone far from me?* and ver. 31. *O generation, see ye the word of the Lord. have I been a wilderness unto Israel?* a land of *darkness?* May not the Lord say unto us, as *Pharaoh* did to *Hadad,* 1 King. 11. 22. *What hast thou lacked with me, that behold, thou seekest to go to thine own Country?* Nay, *what could have been done more,* then what the Lord hath done for us? *Isa.5.4.*

How sadly hath the Lord testified against us, because of our
                                                                    loss

loſs of our *firſt love,* and our *remiſsneſs* and negligence in his Work? Why hath the Lord ſmitten us with Blaſting and Mildew now ſeven years together, ſuperadding ſometimes ſevere Drought, ſometimes great Tempeſts, Floods, and ſweeping Rains, that leave no food behinde them? Is it not becauſe the Lords Houſe lyeth waſte? Temple-work in our Hearts, Families, Churches is ſhamefully neglected? What ſhould I make mention of *Signes* in the Heavens and in the Earth, *Blazing-Stars, Earthquakes,* dreadful *Thunders* and *Lightnings,* fearful *Brovings?* What meaneth the heat of his great Anger, in calling home ſo many of his *Ambaſſadors?* In plucking ſuch burning and ſhining *Lights* out of the Candleſticks, the principal *Stakes* out of our Hedges, the *Corner-ſtones* out of our Walls? In removing ſuch faithful *Shepherds* from their Flocks, and breaking down our *defenced Cities, Iron Pillars,* and *Brazen-Walls?* Seemeth it a ſmall thing unto us, that ſo many of Gods *Prophets* (whoſe Miniſtry we came into the Wilderneſs to enjoy) are taken from us in ſo ſhort a time? Is it not a Sign that God is making a way for his Wrath, when he removes his *Choſen* out of the *Gap?* Doth he not threaten us with a *Famine* of the Word, the *Scattering* of the Flock, the *Breaking* of the Candleſticks, and the turning of the *Songs* of the Temple into *howlings?*

It is high time for us to *remember whence we are fallen, and repent, and do our firſt Works.* Wherefore let us *lift up the hands that hang down, and ſtrengthen the feeble knees, and make ſtraight paths for our feet, leſt that which is lame be turned out of the way, but let it rather be healed,* Heb 12. 12, 13. Labour we to redreſs our Faintings and Swervings, and addreſs our ſelves to the Work of the Lord. Let us ariſe and build, and the Lord will be with us, and from this day will he bleſs us.

Alas, we are feeble and impotent; our hands are withered, and our ſtrength dried up.

Remember the man that had a withered hand: Chriſt

D ſaith

saith unto him, *Stretch forth thy hand,* and he stretched it forth, *and it was restored whole, like as the other,* Mat. 12. 13. How could he stretch forth his hand, when it was withered, the Blood and Spirits dried up, and the Nerves and Sinews shrunk up? The Almighty Power of Christ accompanying his Command, enabled the man to stretch forth his withered hand, and in stretching it forth, restored it whole, like as the other. Where the Soveraignty of Christ's Command takes place in the Conscience, there is effectual grace accompanying it to the healing of our Spiritual Feebleness and Impotency, and the enabling of us to perform the duty incumbent on us. Though we have no might, no strength, yet at Christ's Command, make an essay. Where the word of a King is, there is power.

But alas, our Bruise is incurable and our Wound grievous, there is none to repair the Breach, there is no healing Medicine.

The Lord Jesus, the great Physician of *Israel*, hath undertaken the Cure. *I will restore health unto thee, and I will heal thee of thy wounds, saith the Lord,* Jer. 30 17. No case is to be accounted desperate or incurable, which Christ takes in hand. If he undertake to heal *Jairus* his daughter, he will have her *death* esteemed but *a sleep,* in reference to his power. *She is not dead, but sleepeth,* Mat. 9. 24. When Christ came to *Lazarus* his grave, and bade them take away the stone, *Martha* saith, *Lord, by this time he stinketh; for he hath been dead four dayes:* But Christ answereth, *Said I not unto thee, that if thou wouldest believe, thou should-st see the glory of God?* *Joh.* 11. 40. Let us give glory to God by believing his word, and we shall have real and experimental manifestations of his *glory* for our good and comfort.

But alas, our hearts are sadly prejudiced against the Means and Instruments, by which we might expect that Christ should cure and heal us.

Were not the hearts of *John's Disciples* leavened with carnal emulation and prejudices against *Christ* himself? They would

would not own him to be the Messias, nor believe their Master's Testimony concerning him: insomuch that the Lord saw it necessary that *John* should decrease and be abased, that *Christ* might encrease and be exalted: and therefore suffered *Herod* to shut up *John* in Prison, and keep him in durance about twelve moneths, and at length to cut off his head, *that so these fondlings might be weaned from their Nurse;* and when *John* was dead, his Disciples resort to Jesus, acquaint him with the calamity that befell them, and were perfectly reconciled to him, passing into his School, and becoming his Disciples, *Mat.* 14 12.

But alas, the Times are difficult and perillous; the Wind is stormy, and the Sea tempestuous, the Vessel heaves and sets, and tumbles up and down in the rough and boisterous waters, and is in danger to be swallowed up.

Well, remember that *the Lord sitteth upon the flood, yea the Lord sitteth King for ever,* Psal. 29 10. *His Way is in the sea, and his path in the great waters, and his footsteps are not known,* Psal. 77. 19. *He stilleth the noise of the seas, the noise of their waves, and the tumult of the people,* Psal. 65. 7. *He saith to the raging Sea, Peace, be still: and the Wind ceaseth, and there is a great calm,* Mark 4. 39. Yea, he can enable his people to tread and walk upon the waters. To sail and swim in the waters, is an easie matter; but to walk upon the waters, as upon a pavement, is an act of wonder. *Peter* at Christ's call *came down out of the ship and walked on the water to go to Jesus,* Matth. 14. 29. and as long as his Faith held, it upheld him from sinking; when his Faith failed, his body sunk: but he *cried to the Lord, and he stretched forth his hand and caught him, and said unto him, O thou of little faith, wherefore didst thou doubt?*

But what shall we do for bread? The encrease of the field and the labour of the Husbandman fails.

Hear Christ's answer to his Disciples, when they were troubled, because there was but one Loaf in the ship. *O ye of little faith, why reason ye, because you have no bread?*

perhaps

perceive ye not yet, neither understand? have ye your heart yet hardened? having eyes, see ye not? and having ears, hear ye not, and do ye not remember? *Mark* 8. 17, 18.—*Mat.* 16. 8, 9. Those which have had large and plentiful experience of the grace and power of Christ in providing for their outward Sustenance, and relieving of their Necessities, when ordinary and usual Means have failed, are worthy to be severely reprehended, if afterward they grow anxiously careful and solicitous, because of the defect of outward supplies. In the whole Evangelicall History, I finde not that ever the Lord Jesus did so sharply rebuke his Disciples for any thing, as for that fit and pang of Worldly care and solicitude about Bread. Attend we our Errand, upon which Christ sent us into the Wilderness, and he will provide Bread for us. *Matth.* 6. 33. *Seek ye first the Kingdome of God, and his Righteousness, and all these things shall be added unto you.*

But We have many Adversaries, and they have their subtile Machinations and Contrivances, and how soon we may be surprized, We know not.

Our diligent Attention to the Ministry of the Gospel, is a special means to check and restrain the rage and fury of Adversaries. The people's assiduity in attendance upon Christ's Ministry, was the great obstacle that hindred the execution of the bloody Counsels of the Pharisees. *Luk.* 19. 47, 48. *He taught daily in the Temple, but the chief Priests and the Scribes, and the chief of the people, sought to destroy him, and could not finde what they might do: for all the people were very attentive to hear him.* If the people cleave to the Lord, to his Prophets, and to his Ordinances, it will strike such a fear into the hearts of enemies, that they will be at their wits ends, and not know what to do. However, In this way we have the promise of divine Protection and Preservation. *Revel.* 3. 10. *Because thou hast kept the word of my Patience, I also Will keep thee from the hour of Temptation, which shall come upon all the world, to try them*

that

that dwell upon the earth. Let 'us with *Mary* choose this for our Portion, *To sit at Christ's feet and hear his word*, and whosoever complain against us, the Lord Jesus will plead for us, as he did for her, and say, They *have chosen that good part, which shall not be taken away from them*, *Luk.* 10.42. *A M E N.*

F I N I S.

Pag. 14. line 28. *for* ground *reade* grand.

CPSIA information can be obtained
at www.ICGtesting.com
Printed in the USA
BVHW011016140722
642157BV00009B/131